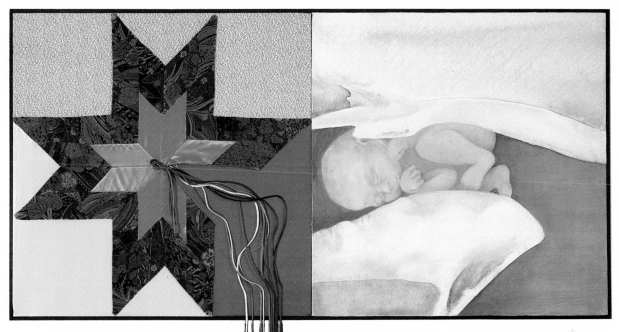

"Beginnings"
by Erma Martin
Yost, 1981, oil
and quilt, 23 x 45
inches. Collection
of the artist.

BORN
GIVING
BIRTH

Edited by
Mary H. Schertz and Phyllis Martens

You are born, giving birth,
a haloed madonna,
the word thrust forth
throws light in your eyes.

—*Barbara Esch Shisler, "Utterance"*

# Born Giving Birth

## Creative Expressions of Women

Edited by Mary H. Schertz
and Phyllis Martens

Faith and Life Press
Newton, Kansas

Printed on recycled paper in the United
States of America.

97   96   95   94   93   92   91

8   7   6   5   4   3   2   1

Library of Congress Number 91-75974
International Standard Book Number
0-87303-148-2

Editorial direction for Faith and Life
Press by Maynard Shelly and Susan E.
Janzen, general editors; copyediting by
Delia Graber and Edna Dyck; design by
John Hiebert; printing by Mennonite
Press.

**Acknowledgements:** "Burden"
and "Enough" by Jean Janzen are from
*Three Mennonite Poets,* Copyright
©1986 by Good Books, Intercourse,
Pennsylvania 17534. All rights
reserved. Used by permission.
"Enough" was published first in
*Yankee,* September 1984.

DEDICATION

**Dedicated** to the Ecumenical Decade of Churches in Solidarity with Women: 1988—1998, launched by the World Council of Churches to provide a framework for addressing the concerns and perspectives of women within the church and the larger society.

A year and a half ago, when Eastern Mennonite College was featuring Mennonite writers during homecoming week, I spoke in assembly about my work as editor of the Christian feminist magazine, *Daughters of Sarah*. A young woman student came to me afterward and told me of her aspirations of becoming a writer. "I used to write poetry," she said, "but I don't anymore. *Everyone* writes poetry—and *nobody* reads it!"

I half agreed with her. I myself have a love/hate relationship with poetry. On one hand, I groan when week after week my office mail contains envelopes thick with verse from fledgling poets. Some is bad poetry; most is not appropriate for the focus of our magazine. Some poems miss the mark by only a hair's breadth—one person on our editorial board has a subjective negative reaction, or at the last minute we have run out of space.

But occasionally a poem arrives that stings the eyes with tears, or elicits a belly laugh, or hones down the thrust of a wordy article we were considering into one-tenth the space. When a poem so profoundly articulates human experience, there is no doubt but that it must be shared in print.

Many of the poems and works of visual art in this volume are of the latter sort, and speak directly to my experience as a Mennonite woman. I spent a kairos moment this morning. Time stood still while I savored poem after poem—slowly, deliciously, my heart kneading stanzas like bread dough, pondering entire images distilled into a few spare lines.

I lingered long with the poems of women I know personally: Muriel Thiessen Stackley, Ellen Kroeker, and Mary Lou Houser. As a student of the Bible, I especially loved the poems that captured an unusual perspective on a biblical woman: a sympathetic view of Lot's wife, the dragging feet of Moses' mother delivering her son to Pharaoh's daughter. Or the feminine aspects of God in the haunting "Night Passages," "Mother Spirit," and "What Is Your Name?"

Poems of flowers and growing plants and of older women, such as "Thieving," "Planting Flowers," "Rooted," and

"Eucharist," along with many visual images, connect specifically with my Mennonite roots. A book like this could never have emerged from my mother's or grandmother's generations. They, like other Mennonite women of their time, poured their creative energies into sewing, quilting, gardening, or lining up bright rows of canned fruit, red beets, and chowchow on shelves in whitewashed cellars. I am so glad a piece of their legacy is passed on through the poetry of their daughters.

There are three ways in which I hope women and men will use this book. First, privately and meditatively—curled up in a chair on a rainy evening gorging on beauty, or tasting one poem or art work at a time in conjunction with biblical poetry in morning devotions.

Second, I would encourage women to gather in small groups to discuss several poems and drawings at a time, so that we can communally claim these works of art as our own. It is true that I and many others living in the age of television sound bites do not often read poetry. I do not have the patience to sit with a poem until it unlocks its secrets to me.

But how I have come to value an hour of poetry read aloud and discussed with other women! Each year the Daughters of Sarah schedule an evening where one of our group introduces us to selected poems by women, or poetry using female imagery. We build on each other's discoveries, and our excitement warms us for days afterward.

Third, we need to read this poetry publicly—in worship services, in Sunday school, at conferences and assemblies, in committee meetings, in women's gatherings. It is a way to counterbalance the many men's voices we hear in our churches, a way to give voice to women so often invisible, in our nurseries and kitchens and children's classrooms of our meetinghouses. No, it is not canon in the strictest sense of the word, but it reflects an important part of our story as the people of God, as Mennonites, and especially as Mennonite women.

*Born Giving Birth* has been ten years in gestation. My hope is that from now on no Mennonite student can say, "*Nobody* reads poetry anymore!"

But I have another hope as well, a dream of another birth in the making. I would like to see Mennonite men relinquishing some of their administrative and pastoral leadership roles to women and taking time to dig deep into their souls, exploring their more feminine sides, to produce another book of poetry and visual art. Sometime before the turn of the century I would like to see *Born Giving Birth: Creative Expressions of Mennonite Men.*

*Reta Halteman Finger*

## PREFACE

That Mennonite women are discovering their voices—in Sunday school classes, on church boards and committees, in pulpits, in college and seminary classes—is both beyond dispute and one clear sign that the Spirit of God is alive and at work in our churches. Women's voices are being heard. They are making statements, asking questions, brainstorming; and emerging delightfully, engagingly, sometimes confoundingly.

However, alongside, underneath, above, and beyond this public voice, Mennonite women are discovering another, more private inner voice. It is more profoundly communal. It emerged from shared silence.

For the spirit so long denied expression in the church did not die. It lived on in quilt designs, flower gardens, and creative relationships. It nurtured the practical arts of nursing, teaching, and hospitality. In a sense, each artist represented in this book, Mennonite woman that she is, is indebted to that abiding silent spirit given flesh by mothers, aunts, grandmothers. In another sense, our voices speaking on paper, film, in ink and paint are redemptive voices: redeeming the silence, giving birth from that silence and witnessing to the spirit that did not die.

That abiding and emerging spirit of Mennonite women is celebrated by Erma Martin Yost's "The Survivor" and by the title of this book (a paraphrase of a line in Barbara Esch Shisler's "Utterance"). In a real sense, we are truly born as we create. For in the rhythms of life, survival and birth and creation are synonymous.

The efforts of the artists represented in this book, as well as those forms of art which could not be contained between two book covers—such as liturgical dance, preaching, or drama—are witnesses to life and also to faith. Struggle, pain, and doubt appear, but in the context of triumph, joy, and trust. Good Friday and Easter are, after all, parts of the same reality. However, according to the sweat and thought of these Mennonite women, the resurrection is the context of the crucifixion, and not the other way around.

We are thankful to the Committee on Women's Concerns of Mennonite Central Committee for its vision in commissioning this project as well as for its ongoing commitment to Mennonite women. This book was born in 1982 when the committee invited women to submit their creative work. The fledgling project had a hopeful spurt of growth with the arrival of many pages of poetry, prose, and art; grew into the shape of a book; faltered, almost died; but was resurrected and brought to maturity. The limits of the book meant that much fine work could not be included—and there is a sense of loss therein.

Mary H. Schertz was the first editor of this collection. Esther Wiens served with her as editorial consultant. Phyllis Martens worked as second editor and Jean Janzen reviewed the poetry.

We hope this book will encourage all of us to give attention to the inner voice, and to share what emerges so that all of us may grow in strength and grace.

●

*Mary H. Schertz*
*Phyllis Martens*

# CONTENTS

# SELF·DISCOVERY

"Highland Bouquet" by Erma Martin Yost, 1984; oil and quilt, 37 x 19 inches. Collection of Daniel and Judyth Katz.

W H A T   I S   T H I S                    I N

# What is this in me?

What is this in me,
This ocean of restless waves,
    crashing against stones;
Washing up weeds,
    dead shells,
    driftwood;
From within my soul,
This quivering agony
    of white foam,
Drifting into nothingness?

Is this the very heart of me
    that hurts like roots torn out
    and forever raw to the wind,
    frayed and battered,
Never to be sunk in rich deep earth
    for a purpose?

Yes, this must be me,
Homeless like the wind
    on a bleak November night,
Moaning through bare trees,
As if it has never known a summer
And will never see a spring;
And yet—bringing snow
    to cover warmly that
Which will someday live.

                *—Cornelia Lehn*

M E ?

15

## Wilma

By faith, brave Wilma
(midst mothering,
milking cows, and feeding mouths
of home and farm)
dared pick up a paintbrush
instead of a dust mop
and birthed new being
in canvas and oil,
passing on the faith
and the courage to create
to her daughters
and their daughters
yet to be.

—*Elizabeth Schmidt*

## A birth record

"A birth record is not evidence of identity"
    (Social Security Office).

Neither I nor my mother assent:
I out of angst with the system;
she for that January bed
forty-five years ago, evidence there
in red and white, the bloodless face
and the wet sheet.

But it's true.
Identity is loose as air,
God's breath somewhere before
dawn, the wind riffling
the waves, sighing through jungles,
swirling in smoky caves.
Congesting,
we breathe as one, poisoning
and blessing each other.
What a mixing of vapors
through the long slow pulse of history.

And quivering in that convulsive mix,
is the cry of the infant lung
to name her intimate name.
The cry uncoils in search of soil
to sustain the fragrant leaf,
to freshen the ancient air.

—*Barbara Esch Shisler*

# The birth of a girl

The head is delivered,
and the worst is over.
Shortly the body follows
with an easy, slippery
    swoosh.

We ascertain that this red and purple infant
    of our lineage
is formed as a bud
to open
and receive the sun.
Shaped as a pool
to store water
off glistening slopes.
This baby is a girl.

She is like me.
I have what I wanted!
A woman-child.
Someone to replace me.

I am put alone in a cold white bed
to heal from this victory.
I find it impossible to sleep.
The baby is a girl.

Will she be angry that I so desired her?
I did not beg; I said it did not matter.
But I longed for her, I admit,
as I dreamed,
hands resting on the huge and noble belly,
canopy of the seed I hoped would flower
female.

She will learn that the choice was not mine.
But will she be surprised
that I wrapped this yearning
around the embryo,
aspired for that tiny universe
the second sex?

Listen, little one,
little woman screaming at the light,
listen.
Neither do I
understand God or history.

(I welcome my death
as I watch you grow.)
The child is washed,
dressed, swaddled,
carried to me at midnight.
My uterus tightens, painfully.

Listen again, little daughter,
I have secrets to tell.
(Lodge them for now in your unused womb.)
You may stand in Eden.
And you may run with greetings
from a long deserted Tomb.

—Dora Dueck

"Seated girl
holding cup" by
Rebecca B. Mast,
drawing

# Periscopic pain

I am battle weary with the war
    you wage upon my spirit.

Like a submarine, you dive beneath
    the surface of yourself hiding, then
    reaching to rise up and torpedo
    me whenever I fail to play
        war games
    on the sea of your inventions.

I've been targeted for years, receiving
    your inner explosions like time bombs
    carefully calculated to find and mark
        the deepest wounds;
    you take my love and say
    "It's false," because you cannot
    control it through your periscope.

How ironic. Moving like a sailboat, I try
    shifting with the winds to rise above
    the subterranean level your ship would
    pull me in.

Look at my sails freely soaring toward the sky.
Let me go and I will sail to you, eventually,
    when the patches mend secure from rips your
    fabricated storms have shorn.

You've been strong—
    a true-blue (well, blue, anyway)
    sailor; but you've had only one
destination—
        your own.
    I look to another shore.

*—Ashley Jo Becker*

# In honour of Mary Martens-Martin

Though time has made her small
and thinned her greying hair,
her grace remains.
Though toil has gnarled her hands
and stooped her shrinking frame,
her strength endures.
So many times she laboured hard:
her womb,
an artifice of new creation;
her breasts,
full vessels of abundant life.

And two generations removed,
I stand before her now,
worlds apart in inclination,
yet drawn into her sphere.
Is it faith that gives her strength,
that lends her body grace
and holds me by her side?

She is
a living sacrifice of love;
and I,
a pale reflection
of her artful procreation.

*—Kathy Shantz*

# Transformational Grandma

Listen carefully, students.

I am an irregular verb.
I am strong.
I do not take the usual endings.
I surprise you instead.

I am to be.

Repeat after me.
I am who I am.
I am who I am.
She is who she is.
She is who she is.
Very good.

Note that regular verbs
Take ordinary endings, i.e.:
        follow, followed
        wither, withered
        stay, stayed
        tie, tied

But other irregular verbs include
        do, did, done
        choose, chose, chosen
        know, knew, known
        lead, led, led.

Practice these diligently.
It will give you something to do
If Dial-a-Prayer is busy.

Learn particularly how to manage the future.
I will do.
I will lead.
Etc.

Note that he and she function identically
Whether singular or plural.
He does, she does, they do.
This, you see, saw, have seen, and will see
Proves that grammar
Is destiny.

Now, students, take a deep breath.
Begin
Begin
Begin
To be.

—*Peggy Newcomer*

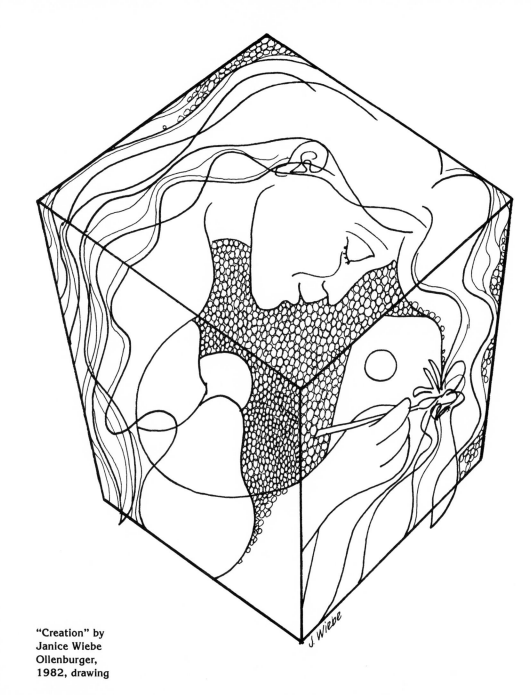

"Creation" by
Janice Wiebe
Ollenburger,
1982, drawing

## Prayer for myself

Let's go in together
I fear echoing darkness
My hollow chamber
holds aborted beings
crouched in corners
piled in writhing heaps
knowing nothing, seeing nothing
waiting for us to hold and heal
and bring to brightest birth

—*Linea Reimer Geiser*

## Expensive Eden

The greenback serpent
Stands subtly behind us
As we spend ourselves
And consume the fruit
To which he points.

Slowly, the knowledge
Of good and evil grows
In self-centeredside
And full bellied, we ache,
Knowing our souls are naked.

—*Ruth Naylor*

# CHILDHOOD

S H E   S T R E T C H E S

"Childhood" by Erma Martin Yost, 1981, oil and quilt, 51 x 63 inches. Private collection.

## Floral supremacy

When I was ten, a bantam weight on long
summer creaks
from shadeporch chains of slatback
swinging,
munching saltbread soft,
I rubbed the cool
Indian-beaded curtains from my eyes
and steamed my breath on leaded glass
Rose Stover skies
cloudbeaked by rain hosed down in Hebrew.

ARMS TO WINDY SPRING · WILD SKY

I didn't know that girls
would have to walk three yards behind,
that only men could grow to be the boy
Master Painters.
So I swept my contrapuntal themes
through forms and colors past the whys
and all protesting,
accepting textured missions only
from dimensions
where there are no lies.

—*Sylvia Gross Bubalo*

23

"I am a child of
the universe" by
Sylvia Gross
Bubalo, 1977,
drawing

24

## A cross to fly

Slight cross of feather-weighted wood,
Some twisted string perimeters
The fragile slotted ends.
Brown paper. Paste.
A tail of faded cotton tied,
And yards and yards of cord
Slip-knotted and secured.
Great dreams are worked to substance
Made to fly.

Big brothers, little sister, find
A furrowed field
Of dark and hardened lumps of earth
That bruise small children's running feet.
The brothers lift their treasured kite
With swiftly straining cord
As high as childhood's arms can reach,
While Sis runs with its ragged tail held high.

"Run faster, Sis!" She stretches arms
To windy spring-wild sky
And stumbles through the bruising earth,
Running her heart out
So their dreams can fly.

—*Fern Pankratz Ruth*

## Mother braids my hair

Mother
quickly braids
my hair.
My skin is tight.

I see her
in the mirror
even now
as I touch
this tumbling mass.
It is like
a ripening field of flax
that spills over slopes
where roses are wild
and corn leaves dance.

I will be late, Mother.
My dress is torn
and stained with grass;
and when you kiss me,
your lips are on the wind.

—*Jean Janzen*

"Preservation IV"
by Mary Lou
Weaver Houser,
drawing

26

## Written for my mother

There is a range of smells, dominated
by sun, dirt, and dry air
that awakens a small animal hibernating
in this casing of a body. I'm snared
by the young child I was in Mother's garden.
Beside me, a tattered bushel basket holds
its weeds, limp and dying, and again
Mother's hands, with that biting scent of marigolds
on them, sweep down and lift me up.
Her face sweats with Kansas heat
but she smiles at the heap of tough
Bermuda grass she has pulled. I feel her heart beat
strong. She sniffs the air with satisfaction.
"Now, my *Jüngste*, for peaches and celebration!"

—*Ellen Kroeker*

## Family reunion

Indoors where
Grandfolks pray,
Bones creak;

Outdoors where
Children play,
Swings squeak.

—*Fern Pankratz Ruth*

"Silenced water"
by Ethel
Abrahams,
serigraph on
hand-made paper

# Garden pump

In Grandma's Eden,
back between the raspberry hedge
and the melon-striped gooseberries,
the old black-iron pump
coughs out well water.

Laughter floats across ripening pea patches
and swaying cornstalks
as bare feet squirm and splash
in the slime-lined dugout.
The old visored knight plays with us—
who can best endure?

The heavy iron mouth
gasps and splutters
an icy challenge;
our curled toes
turn from the delicate pink
of Grandma's *pluma mousse*
to the deepest red
of her choke-cherry jam.
The game is over; I'm the victor.
My feet have endured
longest.

But now my leather-bound feet
approach this spotted pump.
It stands a monument—dark shrine
framed with prim floral decor.
But it is bulky and unkempt
in our freshly-mown yard
imprisoned in its fresh cement plot.
The old knight's squeaky lance
is frozen in stilled air,
and its rust-rimmed mouth
has run dry.

—*Frances Martens Friesen*

# SEXUALITY

Y O U  A R E

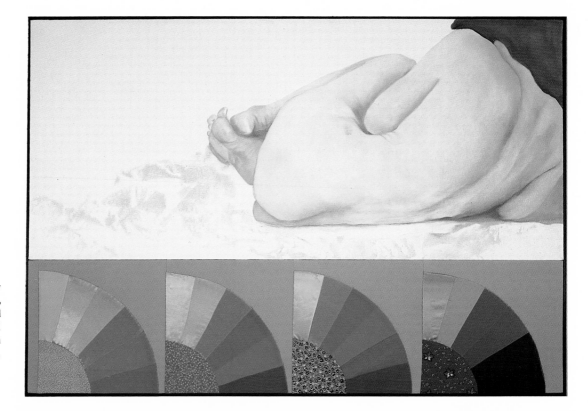

"First love" by
Erma Martin Yost,
1981, oil and
quilt, 35 x 51
inches. Collection
of the artist.

## Another element

Sometimes in your arms
this falling through space,
this spinning,
stops,
and what was old
becomes new,
a fragile moment
that catches us
like a net.

T H E   P O E M   O F   L E A V I N G   A N D   C L E A V I N G

Our lives in
relentless motion.
But sometimes
when we kiss
we are in
another element.
Not a halting
of the clock,
but a cutting
through, our love
in conjunction, perhaps,
with light. Sometimes
in a glance, or
your fingertips
resting
on my shoulder.

—*Jean Janzen*

## Wedding poem

You
are the poem God wrote,
when he created
Adam and Eve
in the Garden,
and that is why
you leave
mother and father
and are united
and become
one flesh.

You
are the poem Christ wrote,
when he came
to earth.
Within you,
in the love of each for each,
is the longing
for the love
that made him
walk among us,
to his death.

You
are the poem
of leaving and cleaving;
and in you
the world is created,
and in you
the Savior is born
and crucified,
and in you,
today and always,
he conquers death.

*—Cathy Conrad*

## Poema Matrimonial

Ustedes son el poema
que escribió Dios
cuando creó
a Adán y Eva
en el huerto,
y por eso
dejan a sus padres
y se unen
y se hacen
una sola carne.

Ustedes son el poema
que escribió Jesús
cuando vino
a la tierra.
Dentro de ustedes,
en el amor de uno para otra,
es el anhelo del amor
que le hizo andar
entre nosotros
hacia la muerte.

Ustedes son el poema
de dejar y juntar;
y por ustedes
se crea el mundo,
y por ustedes
se nace y muere
el Salvador,
y por ustedes,
hoy y siempre,
vence a la muerte.

*—Cathy Conrad*

"Young woman"
by Rebecca B.
Mast, drawing

## Painted philosophic conflict

It's a long long way
From the Sailors' Quarter
To Rijksmuseum
In Amsterdam

And though the profession
Of the Quarter
Was born long before
Rembrandt van Rijn
Or his "Jewish Bride,"
The rebellion of mind
Against commitment
To others or Mosaic law
Is spray painted
On structures that line
The streets and canals between.

Red-lighted windows
Display female merchandise;
Satisfaction can be purchased
In just a few moments
And you'll be free:
No responsibility; no disease.
There'll be no cameras
Or whispers to tell. After all,
Who reports the consumer
Grocery shopping
To fill his appetites?

This poem is a graffiti
Of its own, but the lines
Of internal argument
Were set aside at the museum,
Not to be publicly splattered—
Respecting different opinions
And dignity commanded
Since civilization began. But

Rembrandt picked up my thoughts;
He brushed them softly
Into a wordless masterpiece.
The Jewish bride is protected,
Cared for.
Tenderness is oiled
Into every line.
This is the wedding of lives
Between a man and the woman
He loves.

I bought a canvas copy
For my son.
—Ruth Naylor

34

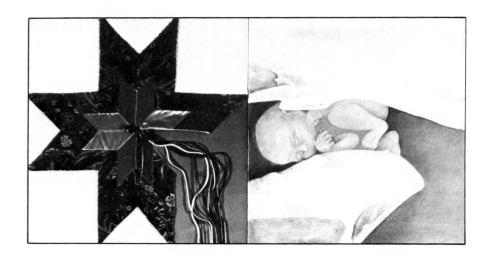

"Beginnings" by
Erma Martin Yost,
1981, oil and
quilt, 23 x 45
inches. Collection
of the artist.

## Woman song

Oh I am fertile.
    The good seed grows
In a secret manner
    Which no man knows.

The stars were spinning
    When we embraced.
With ancient rhythm
    The seed was placed.

Now I am sluggish
    And slow as a clod,
But a green shoot growing
    Will pierce the sod.

Oh I am fertile.
    The good seed grows
In a secret manner
    Which no man knows.

*—Elaine Sommers Rich*

# NURTURING

YOU   SERVE

"Madonna and child" by Erma Martin Yost, 1981, oil and quilt, 50 x 72 inches. Private collection.

T H E M   S I L E N T L Y

# He needs my hand to hold

I heard my little one's plaintive call,
"Please make me a bathtub lake
or a little ginger cake,
and let's tuck Teddy in bed
and go outside for a ride
on my sled."
I ache to be alone,
to read a book
or write a poem,
but I will wait until he sleeps.
I will wait until he sleeps.

And really when I think of it,
he's closer to the earth than I.
There will be a star-shaped flower,
an April shower
and sloshing puddles
and finger paint muddles,
and he needs my hand to hold
sometimes,
he needs my hand to hold.

*—Geraldine Harder*

## Fragrance filled the house

Aganetha—child of God—
a quiet life she led.
No one ever paid much mind
to what she did or said.

Aganetha wed, and bred
a child or two or three—
not too good and not too bad—
for all the world to see.

Aganetha helped her spouse.
She stayed right by his side.
It never came into her mind
to reprimand or chide.

When it was time for her to die
she mixed a batch of bread.
She put the loaves into the stove
and lay down on her bed.

Her heart stopped beating easily.
Her husband found the bread.
And when he came to where she lay
he saw that she was dead.

Aganetha—child of God—
a quiet life she led.
But now we tell and tell and tell
of Aganetha's bread.

—*Muriel Thiessen Stackley*

## Burden

"The light draws off
As easily as though no one could die
Tomorrow." —*Christopher Fry*

Evening sets down a tinted
glass dome on the rim of the world,
and once again you stand
in the doorway calling the children
to supper. One more game, they cry
with voices that splay the air, then
a quick scramble and silence as they
hide in the hedge. You lean heavily
on the door frame watching the light
change. Late bird calls, stillness,
the ash leaves shiver.

The children huddle closer, their toes
pressing into the fine dust. They cover
their mouths to stifle the sound
of their breathing. They stiffen
with expectation.

And then it is dark. You gather them
into the bright square of the kitchen.
You serve them silently, but you long
to expel a great cry: oh my darlings
with the golden hair, with eyes clear
as water, with your small dark seeds,
deep and divided.

—*Jean Janzen*

## Utterance

"May I help you?"
I wait—and you enter
the Gethsemane of speech.

Your body contorts, arms
thrash at imprisoned signals.
Saliva spurts, eyes
purse with each spasmed sound.
Sweat oozes like blood
at the wrenched agony
of utterance.

I do not dare to help you.
Language makes, as it is made.
You are born, giving birth,
a haloed madonna,
the word thrust forth
throws light in your eyes.

And still you must know
the dark passion of the garden,
where swords slash at our ears,
and words echo in trees;
where life is made whole
in the lonely, laboring night.

—*Barbara Esch Shisler*

"Credo" by Janice
Wiebe Ollenburger,
drawing, 1986

39

# To Margaret Friesen

[In December 1976, a story appeared in the
Windsor (Ont.) *Star* describing the sentencing
of a twenty-six-year-old Mennonite woman
to three months in a psychiatric institute
for beating her fifteen-day-old baby to
death with a baby bottle. Upon her release,
she was to serve nine months probation
even if she returned to her native Mexico.
The report said simply, "Mrs. Friesen was
described as having had a difficult life,
raising seven children in seven years."]

Your whispers of despair
Unheard amidst the groans
Of childbirth

Burst forth in a
Final frenzied shriek of anguish.

Seven children in seven years,
And only a child yourself.

Demented, torn,
Wasted before your life began,
You walked, in your woman's way,
To the edge of hell.

You are not alone—

The centuries have borne
The shrieks and curses
Of demanded mother-love.

Of you,
Too much has been required.

I thought the world was different now.

—*Margaret Loewen Reimer, 1977*

**"Monday a.m." by
Mary Lou Weaver
Houser, print**

## In the house of my pilgrimage

(Psalm 119:54)

There are not many steps
forth, forth, and back,
in this house of my pilgrimage:
it's a small place.
The floors are beige,
the walls flat white,
they muffle the shadows,
blur day and night.

From the kitchen to the bedrooms,
sofa to the hall,
daily and endlessly I travel
this plain where I cook,
draw water, enfold children.
These rooms, my camp;
this carpet, my path.
I look to horizons
in carefully framed and treasured pictures.

Here I utter my complaints,
eat God's patience as a brown spotted quail,
sing in a windowless kitchen
the songs of ascents.

—Dora Dueck

## Parable of the self-sacrificial mother

A mother came to him, saying,
Teacher, what good deed must I
do
to inherit the kingdom?
I have kept the commandments,
I have sold all my belongings
and given to the poor,
I have served God and family
with all of my being—
what do I still lack?
And he said to her,
Woman, love thyself.

—Elizabeth Schmidt

41

"Seated woman 1"
by Rebecca B.
Mast, drawing

# Lot's wife

Hello.
It's really a pleasure to be here today.
It's about time I told you *my* half of the story.
Most people know me as Lot's wife.

Lot and I were married in Canaan on my
twenty-first birthday.
We had a tough time at first.
I doubt we'd have made it without Lot's
Uncle Abram's help.
Life was a struggle—
Anyway, just as we got things under control
and could eat two good meals a day,
along came a famine
and wiped out nearly everything we had.

Abram and Lot decided to truck on down
to Egypt for a while to wait the famine out.
I packed up our meager belongings
and off we went.
Egypt was pretty good to us.
The herds grew and multiplied.
We prospered as well; but, you know how it goes,
it just wasn't home.
So, after a few years,
we packed up again and headed back to Canaan.

Once we arrived, it was obvious something
had to be done.
Lot's and Abram's herdsmen were bickering
back and forth.
And well, to tell you the truth,
Lot and I were ready to have some time
by ourselves—cut the umbilical
cord with Abram and Sarah for once.
So, when Abram suggested the two households split,
Lot and I decided it was a great idea.

Lot chose the fertile Plains of Jordan,
leaving Abram dry old Canaan.
Now as selfish as this sounds,
I'd just like you to understand the situation.
Abram and Sarah were getting along in years
and had enough wealth to support them
for the rest of their lives.
Sarah was well beyond childbearing age
and it would be a miracle if she'd
ever conceive.
Lot and I were just starting our family—
our first daughter was two and I was
carrying the second at the time; so, of course,
I was glad when Lot chose the plains.
I felt sure we'd settle and prosper here,
once and for all!
And we did. In the city of Sodom.

How good it felt to finally put down
some roots!
This was the first time since my marriage
that I could actually organize my
household efficiently.
The herds grew and Lot often brought me
presents of imported silk and jewelry.
I watched my daughters grow into
beautiful young women.
I kept a lovely garden behind the house,
which I tended every day.
I often visited with friends who lived nearby.
Of course, Sodom had its problems as most
large cities do,
but it was all a matter of whom you associated
with.

Everything was going fine.
Everything, that is,
until those two angels showed up.
Lot let them in one night
and gave them some food.
These angels said they had come from God
with a message.
"Flee for your lives," they said next day, "and
don't look back.
The Lord is going to destroy the city."
Oh, great, I thought.
Here we go again!
I dreaded the thought of packing up again
and heading off across the plains.
When would this stop?
My home,
my friends,
my garden.
I nearly broke down and wept.

The angels seemed pretty urgent about
the whole matter and gave us only
a few minutes to pack.
A few minutes!

How was I supposed to organize myself
in such a short time!
Here I am frantically running around
instructing the servants to load the donkeys
with this and that, while these angels
are continually pressing me to hurry up!
Lot was already on his way down the street
with my two daughters following behind,
so I threw one last golden vessel into
the donkey's basket
and ran to catch up.
Just as they reached the city gates
I fell in line.

"Flee for your lives
and don't look back."
(*Two angels chant in the background.)
"Why, Lord?" I moaned.
"Why this constant fleeing?
Can't you just let me put some roots
down for once? I've worked and struggled
most of my life! Finally, things seem to
be going okay and now this!"
    "Flee for your lives"
(Voices chant, increase intensity.)
My friends,
my garden,
my home.
The jewels, vases, and tapestries.
All left behind!
The gifts from friends in Egypt.
The linen cloth from my mother.
All gone.
So much—
No time—
So much I forgot!
And, here, I am fleeing for my life!
Oh Sodom!
A rough city; yes, Lord; but my home!
Oh Sodom, I shall miss you.
Ahead, I see Lot and my two daughters.
    "And don't look back."
But my home, my friends, my roots!
    "And don't look back."

*Angel voices
chant faintly in
background and
build with rhythm
and intensity,
shouting out
quoted lines at end.

I feel them tearing away.
Something is breaking apart within me,
breaking and bleeding.
 *"And don't look back."*
One last look, Lord!
That's all I ask.

One last look at all that once was.
 "And don't look back" (*Louder*).
Please Lord!
Just one look!
 "And don't look back" (*Still louder*).
That's all I ask, Lord,
 just one. . . .
(*Hands up in pleading position, anguish on face,
slowly turns head over shoulder with last line and
freezes midsentence.*)

       *—Brenda Shantz Broussard*

# And the child grew

"And the child grew, and she brought him to Pharaoh's daughter. . ." (Exod. 2:10, Revised Standard Version).

My feet drag slowly
While the moments fly
Like sinister barbarians
Quick stealing in the night
Last vestiges of anything I
Lived or hoped for.
If this fragile day could stop and
Everything be different
How well life's garment would befit me.
I could wear it graciously,
Head high
Stretching for the sky
Life-filled.

Stop, day!
Stop now and let me listen
To the sound of little feet
On sand,
Minuscule beside my thick, work-hardened ones.
Let me taste this last light moment
Of child hand in mine, etching chunky shape
Into the recess of my mind.
Let me hear the wonder in his voice
And laughter spilling in the grass;
One who does not know what bondage is
Or why.
And let me touch the soft silk curls of innocence
Before I say, "Good-bye."

Good-bye, little Moses
Son.

"And the child grew, and she brought him to Pharaoh's daughter."

—*Anne Neufeld Rupp*

# Night passages

(John 3:1-15; 18:39)

When you came by night
(as I come, soul weary,
a barren womb
longing to be filled),
you thought you knew something,
your search stretched out behind you
like live entrails—
a life long of asking
and answering
and treading on ancient stones
set before and behind
for the building
of a solid edifice.

You thought you knew something
(as I know
filling my life
with empty expectations,
vain labour,
and no relief of birth in sight),
and it was hard to think
of leaving all that
to go where the wind blows,
to travel that wordless, screaming passage
and risk remembering
what memory mercifully declines to recall.

But you risked it, Nicodemus.
And in the bloody afterbirth,
when he was lifted up,
you brought a cradleful of spices.

Was it something he said,
a sign more sure
than the wisdom of sages?
Or did you simply long
as I do,
hearing the sound of that sweet wind,
to enter its streams and be blown through,
swept clean
to dress this weary world anew?

—*Lorraine E. Matties*

# NATURE

R A I N B O W   C O L O R S

"Lilies II" by
Erma Martin Yost,
1985, oil and
quilt, 37 x 19
inches. Collection
of Michael and
Susan
Christophel.

THE SUN PATH

## By the shimmering sea

In the hush of the morn
by the shimmering sea,
there's a blue cloud of mist
and a shore that is kissed
by the waves dancing in.
There's a movement of wings
and a clear call that sings
of a lone gull at peace.
There's a blanket of sand
and a shell treasure land
so clean from the washing
when the quiet day breaks.

In the hush of the eve
by the shimmering sea,
there are rainbow colors
on the sun paths fading,
on the wavelets rippling,
on the smooth sand washing,
and God's benediction
when the quiet night falls.

—*Geraldine Harder*

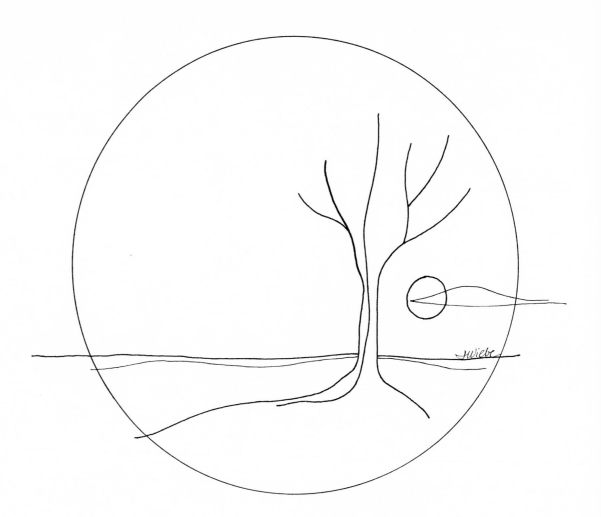

"Solitary
Sentinel" by
Janice Wiebe
Ollenburger,
drawing, 1985

# Climbing Annapurna

(For a team of women in the
Himalayas, 1978)

The mountain juts up, a steeple
stabbing the sky. The sun breaks
behind it, silver and blue, a holy
city. They set out on the last
stretch, and the reach
to the summit.

Fear splits a crevasse
between them, black and bottomless.
They climb on its rim,
extremity tightens their tendons.
They are bound together,
the rope shudders
with the ax and crampons and stakes.

Dread is the rage
of avalanche. They watch
it wipe out the camp, cling
like flecks to their ledge,
go on at the stopped tremor

past fury's caught place caught
frozen. The fallen
Vera and Allison roped together
What thoughts hurtling what
truth two thousand feet down
fused to implacable deep.

Above a bird whirling free
and they too rising
       seeing
          knowing
the world swung full
the God view flung
glory like dream yield
glory for ever more
mountain of the eternal city
    holy      holy
       holy

—*Barbara Esch Shisler*

# Planting flowers

Giving birth.
It's the only sort
I'll ever want to offer—
To dig holes
Dirt thick under my nails.
These stringy roots will tap deep, bloom
And seed so effortlessly.
Behind me
The row of roses
Their heads heavy with Tuesday's rain
Dying against the wooden fence—
I will let them dry and
Bring them in to use
On a bare wreath.
I snip
The dead daisies
Pale, dull heads
And carry them
To the side of the house
Where fall's leaves,
Ends of cucumbers,
Tops of tomatoes,
Peelings of carrots, potatoes,
Crusts of wheat bread
Decay and replenish the soil.
Sometime on a silent evening
Such as this
I will take time
To join them
And I begin to think
Which body part of mine,
Arm, leg, foot
Will be the best fertilizer.

—*Kristen Balzer*

**"Schefflera" by
Fern E. Clemmer,
paper cutting**

Look how these lilies droop you say,
begonias are best in the shade and these
perfect pansies trembling
sedately in the wind's breath.

When there's nothing left to tell
we review the world from a bench
in the elm trees' shade, follow the smooth
half-orbit of frisbees, joggers'
footfalls on dry grass.

Licking ice cream from our fingers
we fish for the last bits of popcorn
as if there will be no more and you
reach for your shawl and say
there's a cool wind
hadn't we best be going.

*—Sarah Klassen*

# SOCIETY

A L O N G   T H E   B U S Y

"Red Sky" by
Erma Martin Yost,
1982, oil and
quilt, 80 x 40
inches. Collection
of Rockingham
Memorial
Hospital.

STREETS THEY STAKE THEIR CLAIM

## Love

reached out
to swab a
wounded
writhing
world.
Risking
contamination
it was
no longer
sterile.

*—Ruth Naylor*

## Limosna

Along the busy streets they stake their claim:
Here sits a young girl, infant at her breast,
And there a hunchbacked ancient, chin to chest,
Their cupped hands limp, their dull eyes blurred with shame.
They've lost their faces and forgot their names,
Abandoned wholly to that burning quest
For sustenance. Passing with the rest,
I note their soiled rags, their fleshless frames.

And then I think of Peter and of John,
Who said, "Of gold and silver we have none.
But here, oh cripple! Take my hand! Arise!"
Then left, and left him dancing in the sun.
But I have not the means to end your sighs.
I toss you pesos with averted eyes.

—Cathy Conrad

## The emigrant's lament

We had heard of plums but could not imagine
the tautness of the purple skin, the lush
yellow fruit inside. As we grew, we believed in plums
less and thought father a master of fiction.
He became silent, his past ruffled to his own eyes
like a lake by a sharp breeze. Father left us
to draw his future in his fears long before they ever
came for him. Their coming was a worn classic, the knock,
the demand, his long look at us, trying to imprint
our faces on his uneasy memory.
We too left, Sonia and I, going the opposite
direction. Our mother waits like a barren tree
of November, all soft growth stripped by the chapping
winds and, though we have had our plums,
what else have we? We are blown like leaves,
scattering and decaying before the winter snow.

—*Ellen Kroeker*

"Indian girl with child" by Naomi E. Engle, drawing

Glory to God!

# Uprooted

Their sorrow whispers
like wind through pine trees.
The old Indian moans
for his lover,
young ones mourn the hollowness
in their bones.

—*Shari Miller Wagner*

# War-tax conflict

broken words
    strewn about the landscape

disquiet
    sweeps across the verbiage
        shifting paralysis heart-to-heart.

*In the beginning was the Word.*

speak now to our warring madness;
whisper wholeness to the debris—
    broken words shielding
    broken bodies.

—*Mary Lou Weaver Houser*

## Jungle rhythms

Hindsight, foresight
See a world that's uptight
Outsight, insight
Hold your own with armed
might
Live right, aim right
Shield thy self and birthright
Insight, outsight
We're so sure that we're right
Foresight, hindsight
Dance around the bomb site!

—*Ruth Naylor*

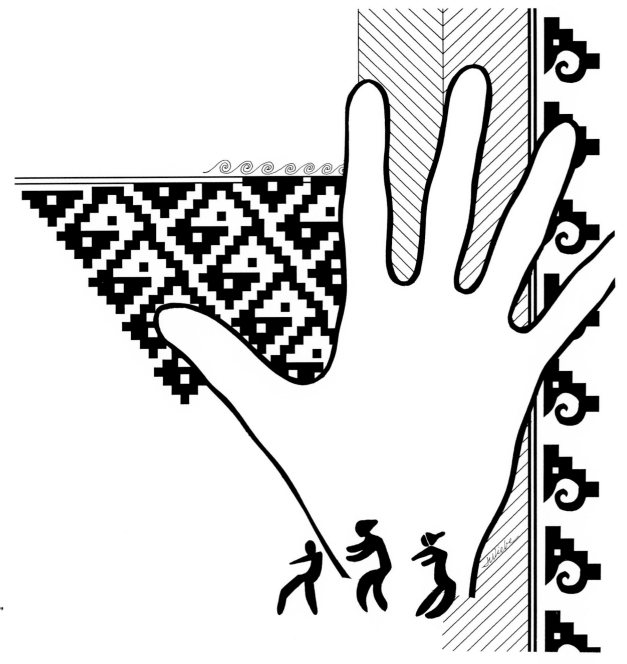

"Fabricatio mundi"
by Janice Wiebe
Ollenburger,
mixed media

# FRIENDSHIP
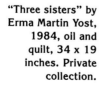

I SEE IN MUDDY RICH

"Three sisters" by Erma Martin Yost, 1984, oil and quilt, 34 x 19 inches. Private collection.

## For Rachel sipping coffee in mug marked H

Coffee cups creep in aromas
  of chocolate pleasures,
    burning tongues where we sipped
    moments of hot truths,
    warm memories, and bitter
      herbs.

Without cream, we take it as it comes,
      ked
     r     or
    e         d
   p          r
              i
           p
            p
              ed or
                  instant joy!

Each has its earthy flavor, each its
  measure full of slow, delicious death.

Sipping slowly, searchingly, I see in
  muddy rich water, a friendship brim
  full, cooled, scorched, and tasted.

Instant coffee is timely, practical, even
              savory

in its quick adaptation; but give me the
natural bean, ground carefully, thoughtfully,
  s l o w l y; it contains a box of friendship
grains, unmeasurable in any coffee cup.

    Creeping s e p a r a t e n e s s
      overcome with cup in hand, lettered

      "H"

          —Ashley Jo Becker

W A T E R   A   F R I E N D S H I P

The Lord Of Hopi
Into the den of men goes the Spirit.
Upon men's nostrils blows the wind
And the men stand and sway
according to the bend of the
Spirit...
S.G.B.

according To The Bend Of The Wind

Sylvia G. Bubalo 6·5·1978

"According to the
bend of the wind"
by Sylvia Gross
Bubalo, 1978

## Running in place

A chilling glance flicked through your mask.
The serpent lurks there still
after ten years of relating
and growing and loving, too.
Our first uneasy truce
clings to present reality,
my bravado and your servility
supplying each other's needs
in strange neurotic patterns.
We are on a treadmill
while I imagined we had arrived
since we both stepped so lively and so high.

—*Linea Reimer Geiser*

## La Primavera

long-mute and dormant,
lacking verbs in which to live
and words to speak my story,
springtime stirred
when a sister brought words
and showers of stories
and spoke my experience
into blossoming becoming.

—*Elizabeth Schmidt*

## To Jane, who is dying

Today in rare solitude
I closed my heart
because it seemed
that God's was closed.

On this March prairie
morning,
in mile after mile of
deafness,
my head was gradually
pierced
by the shrieking song
of meadowlark after
meadowlark.

Persistent in
affirmation
against a steel sky,
they forced me, finally,
to notice them—
one on a fence wire,
one on a road sign,
one on a tree branch,
mouths open in song
(one tongue
silhouetted,
trembling)
aimed at my
passage—
lingering song.

Finally, the admission:
If God knows about
meadowlarks
then God knows about
you.

There is that in
yielding
which bears freedom.
There is that in
relinquishment
which bears
acquisition.
But in your death,
Jane,
I will see no earthly
reason.

—*Muriel Thiessen Stackley*

## I never know my neighbors at the bath

There is a Japanese style of foot-washing practiced at the public bath. You will never know your neighbor until you are allowed to do it.

I have heard that there are some foreigners in Japan, where I live, who have never gone to the public bath. They don't know what they are missing. Thinking about these people, I once offhandedly asked a friend, "Are there *Japanese*, who have never gone to the public bath?" "Oh yes," replied the friend. "My grandmother never went. She lived in Akita prefecture and claimed some noble lineage and considered herself too high-class to go."

There is something middle-class, democratic even, about a public bathhouse. When you peel off clothing and leave it in the cubbyhole in the dressing room and enter the steaming, high-ceilinged bathing room, skin becomes the common denominator. Stripped of apparel's idiosyncrasies, squatting or kneeling in their birthday suits, my neighbors at the bath do not look at all familiar. True, I am not required to speak to anyone, but while I'm rinsing off, someone is certain to sidle up close and, pouring and splashing, start a liquid conversation. Stare as I will I can't figure her out with her permanent hanging in drippy ringlets about her face. Minus glasses, a cane or the perpetual apron, the hairstyle or jogging suit that makes my neighbors human and gives them identity, I am at a loss to know who they are.

Bad as it is not to be able to place faces at the bath, there is another Japanese bathing conundrum. Almost every time I go to the bath, some kind, unknown woman kneels down beside me and offers, "May I wash your back?" And I murmur, "Oh no, you really shouldn't"; but she does it anyway and it feels good. And, then, of course, I say, "And now let me wash your back, please." But she always replies, "Oh no, you don't need to," or "Oh no, my friend just did it," and scoots away on the slippery floor. *They* exchange back washings—why am I never allowed to scrub another woman's back? Is there some conspiracy that doesn't permit foreigners to wash Japanese?

But recently a remarkable thing happened. A woman who said she had seen me in the neighborhood many times (I didn't recognize her, of course) struck up a conversation as we floated under the waterfall in the big tub. It exhausted me to talk to this person I probably knew, but we had a good conversation anyway. She said she went to the public bath once a day—it was her recreation. I told her that when I came to Japan twenty-seven years ago, the public bath fee was nineteen yen a person. Now it is 250 yen a head, and "I can't afford that kind of daily recreation, but I think it is a lovely idea."

And then this neighbor washed my back (surely the hundredth unrequited back washing for me in Japan, I was thinking). She almost peeled the skin off with her plastic sponge, but it felt great. Rather absently, I wondered out loud if I could wash her back. "Oh yes," she said. I washed a Japanese woman's back! A kind of impromptu finale: I, who have received so much from the Japanese all these years, at last, in one symbolic gesture was able to give something back.
                                                —*Mary Cender Miller*

## For Tante Helene

Your ancient ways
Did not conform
To present situations
And I spun Marxist
Threads
In your Kaiser-cloth
You quoted Goethe
And I spoke of Rosa
Yet
Our lives crossed
Interwoven
Stretched through
time
And though
Your ancient ways
Did not conform
We loved

                    —*Kathy Shantz*

CHURCH

I LAND

"Angel Arch" by
Erma Martin Yost,
1984, oil and
quilt, 24 x 48
inches. Collection
of Dr. Melvin and
Dot Keim.

## What is Your name?

I scramble
through ancient words
and faded images

I scream
"What is Your name?"

A G A I N  O N  Y O U R  O U T S T R E T C H E D  W I N G S

for all the names
are sprouting beards
all the pronouns
squeeze to death
Your other reality
my only reality

Ah, Mother Eagle
brooding hovering
toss me up gently
so I land again
on Your outstretched wings

—*Linea Reimer Geiser*

# Mother Spirit

(The original biblical text
sometimes
uses the feminine gender for
God and Spirit.)

Perhaps it was she
with blue wings
and flames in her eyes

before my conception
over the grey face
of my waters, even

as man and woman
dared to touch hands
across a table.

At the first burst
of goodness, at every
movement toward truth,

is she present,
strengthening, brooding,
as cell meets cell

where death sits poised
to seize the perimeters?
Tubal journeys, all

our tenuous attachments,
and her wings dip over
to the quick pulse?

Bright One, then is it you
who entered Sara's laughter
with a shout, you

who groans for me,
who sweeps and strides
in me, who sizzles in my hair?

Lioness, with your rough
licking tongue, light
in your wakeful eyes.

—*Jean Janzen*

**"Scene from
Mennonite World
Conference,
Wichita" by Mary
Lou Cummings,
1978, drawing**

# When

Women
   learn

in silence

men
   pray

lifting holy hands

   a woman
      like a man
         has nothing to say
      until she has surrendered
to the

Only

I
   haven't
quite
      surrendered
yet

have we?

    *—Hedy Leonora Martens*

"Martha Convent's cap strings keep blowing in the wind" by Sylvia Gross Bubalo, 1978, drawing

## The exclusive word

Today
my heart
and mind
grow weary
of *His* Word.
Written and
interpreted
by men,
the language
is for *them*.
Will ever
come the day
decoding
is not needed
for including
me?

—*Nancy S. Lapp, 1980*

# Spaced out on Andrewbaptist Herstory

When the queendom comes
the servants of Jesusan will be
Suderwoman and Klaassdaughter and Kauffwoman
and they'll break off into the
New Womennonite Church
and the Mennonite Sistern

After a while they'll all shuffle up again and
Just settle down to being
Leatherpeople and Frieschildren and Hoffolk
In the Congregation of the Simple Lifestyle Unisex Spirit

—*Peggy Newcomer*

# AGING, DEATH, RESURRECTION

YOU  STEP  WITH

"The Survivor" by Erma Martin Yost, 1981, oil and quilt, 51 x 41 inches. Private collection.

78

## Rooted

My old mother stands rooted
in her garden. Past green
peppers and watercress
bent like one of her hairpins
both ends touching earth.
A gray sweater stretched
across thin hips, skirt fluttering
a modest challenge to the night wind.
Maybe she's pulling weeds
or planting parsnips to replace
what cutworms have eaten.

Cutworms if allowed to live
graze their way through
tender bean sprouts, peas
new petunia stems, all this
under cover of dark moist soil
and when they've spoiled
my mother's garden
they'll be transformed into mud-
coloured moths that crawl out of corners
lured by the naked light.

Behind lampshades their vulgar fluttering
drags on and on.

My mother straightens her back
as far as possible, pulls herself
up the steps, removes mud-
covered shoes and when she's washed
the green stains from her fingers
she brings the large Bible
close to the lamp
and with a magnifying glass
pins down these words:
*The body that is sown*

*perishable is raised
imperishable.* Joy fills her eyes
spilling on dry cheeks
a quiet shining
as she prepares for sleep.

—*Sarah Klassen*

"Grandma
Stauffer" by Judy
A. Yoder,
photographs

## Song of the years

I watched you walking up the hill
each leaning toward the other till
it seemed a single body moved—
a single rhythm, singly grooved.
A strange arithmetic you tone
where one and one make only one,
and one subtracted leaves not one
but half a one who's better gone
than left to walk the hill alone.
You step with measured step and
slow—
shoulders stooped, heads bowed low—
arm in arm like hand in glove.
Be you eighty and in love?

—*Muriel Thiessen Stackley*

# Enough

Another evening
folding its wings
among the ash trees,
a wind stirring
the darkening spaces.

My mother asks
did I love you
enough?
She quilts with a very
sharp needle
making tiny close
stitches around
the flying geese
fastening them down
to muslin.

Her hands are becoming
translucent.
Sometimes I see them
float away,
her whole body
becoming loose and free,

but now
the knots, the clipped
threads, the shadows
in the reeds.

—Jean Janzen

# Eucharist

When the silence of four walls
becomes unbearable
my mother attends funerals.
Always funerals
in the gray stone church
beside the wide freeway.

My mother crosses circumspectly
at the lights. Looks both ways.
She can quote you a string of deaths
at this intersection.

Today they bury the old arthritic man
from the high rise.
Last week Mrs. Martin
unnoticed ninety years
was praised and laid to rest.

My mother sits near the back
with other widows, a whole row.
They keep faith-
ful notes of eulogies and roses.
Wipe tears from their eyes.

When they have rejoiced
at one more pilgrim released
from bondage to life
they descend uncertainly, lured
by the lively aroma of coffee

downstairs. Rows of bent hands
curl fervently around warm cups
and break small pieces
of fragrant raisin bread, fresh
from the new bakeshop
on McIvor Mall.

—Sarah Klassen

## For my lost ones

In the silence of the night
I mourn
for my stillborn
children. They
summon me
from an ancient place
eyes wide like the round o
of a soundless cry

I am struck
dumb
yearning in the long-stilled night
for the sound
of any small voice.

—*Lorraine E. Matties*

"Seated woman 2"
by Rebecca B.
Mast, drawing

82

## Leah's time

i

When I was Laban's only child,
   my mother shrank from me. A servant
   watched me; Father's heart was a sea of sand.
   I kept quiet, careful that my noise
   always lay below the wind.
I, the firstborn, was female.
Leah, they called me, meaning wild cow.
   I thrust that name round and round
   in my understanding. A hard pebble.
   No, I never had the exultation
   that wildness stirs.

Mother moved her tent away. I tried
   to find her but the servant grabbed my wrist.
Was I evil? The afternoon lengthened
and Mother's screams grew larger than the sun.
Then a thin cry froze me in my restlessness.
A servant—a woman-servant—knelt before Father,
whispered, "Another one such as she," and pointed
to me. Father howled his anger and kicked sand.

I have long brooded upon this. Many days
   there were when thought slapped thought, furious
   as wind at my tent. What I saw stung me.

ii

Jacob drove us with his herds across these rocky
hills. First, the servants; then, my children
with me. Closest to him, Rachel and her sons.
Rachel worshiped Jacob as her god. She saw only
his robes blowing, his arm giving directions.
Many gods live in these deserts. I watch them, listen
for them, wait for them. I am Leah, the first wife,
the unloved. They called me dull-eyed, but I watched
for all gods, zealous to protect this band
that didn't notice me. I am Leah, the survivor,
the giver of six sons to Jacob.

iii

Now our days are old like worn stones.
   Jacob comes often to my tent. His desire spent on sons,
   he still comes to talk into my silence.
   Yahweh gave him the blessing, Isaac gave him the blessing,
   yet he is filled with longing. Many nights,
   Jacob knits long questions to the stars, thinking I
   am the silent woman who listens, listens with no answers.

Answers birth hard and fast, as sons once did. But I
   nourish them for myself, all this I can now keep for myself.
My eyes explore this face of his that has never seen me.
Who is this Jacob that I should give him succor?
I feed my answers to wind, to sun, to stars
clustered in threes. This desert nurtures me and, in the fury
of blowing sand, comes my exultation.

—*Ellen Kroeker*

# After Borges

*En el tiempo hubo un dia que apago los ultimos ojos
que vieron a Cristo.* There was a day when the last
eyes to have seen Christ closed. —Jorge Luis
Borges, "El testigo."

Was it, perhaps, the old man, the Divine,
Who lived in lonely exile on his island,
Who tasted and was drunk on heavenly wine
And set down visions with a trembling hand?

Was it a woman who recalled a word,
A miracle performed by him so wise,
One who nurtured what she saw and heard
Until the memory fired her aging eyes?

Was it but an infant brought that day
To see another criminal crucified,
A child still too young to run and play
Who stared uncomprehending as he died?

A world withdrew, no more to be exposed,
The day those last eyes to have seen Christ closed.

—*Cathy Conrad*

# The crown of thorns is blooming

On four inches of unlikely stem
(thorn upon thorn upon thorn)
comes a bud
looking for all the world
like another thorn.

But it will open:
two precise petals, blood red,
perfect and perfectly vulnerable,

Blood, Life, Tears, Joy, Death,
Resurrection. All these.
I marvel that a blossom
(so small a one)
sustains the symbolism
that I desperately suck from it.

Strong it stands
pushed out of vicious
yet sustaining stalk
(thorn upon thorn upon thorn).

*Lord, God of Creation,
The crown of thorns is blooming.*
If it can bloom
then I can live
and sing.

—*Muriel Thiessen Stackley*

# Our artists

**Ethel Abrahams**, North Newton, Kansas, taught art on college level and published *Frakturmalen und Schoenschreiben* (1980). "Art is a peacemaking process," she says; "through it I can make the invisible visible. In working with handmade paper and natural dyes for prints and collages, I am building pieces into a unified structure that, I hope, is making a statement." (28)

**Kristen Balzer** lives in Fresno, California. (52)

**Ashley Jo Becker**, Fresno, California, has been a writer since age ten. "From writing and teaching writing, I discover what I value most in life," she says. "I would only stop writing if I were ready to give up my life. Writing is the holiest thing I do and I am most whole while doing it." (19, 67)

**Brenda Shantz Broussard**, Abbeville, Louisiana, grew up in Waterloo, Ontario, where she shared her work about Lot's wife. Since then, she says, "I too have moved several times, working as a nurse in rural West Africa for three years and in northern Canada." Now working as an obstetrical nurse, she has plans for pursuing a masters degree and raising a family. (43)

**Sylvia Gross Bubalo**, Goshen, Indiana, was born in Doylestown, Pennsylvania. A graduate of Goshen College, she also studied at Mennonite Biblical Seminary and worked with Mennonite Central Committee. At the Art Institute of Chicago, where she studied for three years, she met and married Vladimir Bubalo. They were both painters for many years until he died in 1989. She continues to write poetry. (23, 24, 68, 75)

**Fern E. Clemmer**, Lancaster, Pennsylvania, has served as director of communications at Lancaster Mennonite High School. She and her husband, Dennis, have two daughters and attend Community Mennonite Church, Lancaster. They live in a Christian intentional community (Herrbrook) in a single-family dwelling while the other three families live in a nearby farmhouse. (52)

**Cathy Conrad** grew up in Hesston, Kansas, and attended Hesston and Goshen colleges. Her Study-Service Trimester (SST) experience in Nicaragua stimulated a lasting interest in Latin American literature. She now lives in Albuquerque, New Mexico, with her husband, John Gowdy, and small son, Julian. She is oncology nurse manager at a local hospital. (32, 60, 85)

**Mary Lou Cummings** is a free-lance writer and illustrator from Quakertown, Pennsylvania, who enjoys listening to people's stories. She is author of *Surviving Without Romance* and editor of *Full Circle: Stories of Mennonite Women*. She contributes illustrations to *Story Friends*. (74)

**Dora Dueck**, Winnipeg, Manitoba, is the writer of poetry, articles, and the novel *Under the Still Standing Sun* which won a 1989 Silver Angel Award. She is married and the mother of two boys and a girl. (17, 41)

**Naomi E. Engle** lives in Tulsa, Oklahoma, with her husband, Jesse, and daughter, Anna. With a degree in commercial art from Oral Roberts University, her artwork is squeezed in between mothering, baby-sitting, and sponsoring the church youth group. She is a member of Parkside Mennonite Brethren Church in Tulsa. (62)

**Frances Martens Friesen**, a 1983 graduate of Goshen College, served in China with Mennonite Central Committee and China Educational Exchange from 1986 to 1988 and is now working on a master's degree in literature and writing in Georgetown University. (29)

**Linea Reimer Geiser** writes poetry as part of her inner journey. She has written worship and education materials for adults and children. A writer in the church relations department of Mennonite Board of Missions, she resides with her husband, Leonard, in Goshen, Indiana. (21, 69, 73)

**Geraldine Harder**, North Newton, Kansas, is a homemaker and writer, who enjoys writing for children. She has published a book, *When Apples Are Ripe* and with her husband, Milton, wrote *Christmas Goose*, a children's story about life in a Hutterite colony. (37, 49)

**Mary Lou Weaver Houser**, an art teacher at Lancaster Mennonite High School, is founder of ARTSPIRIT, a group of artists interested in creativity and spirituality. She is co-director of Herrbrook Farm Retreat Cottage and a member of Community Mennonite Church of Lancaster. "My current work," she says, "weaves genealogical research with land preservation issues. This art series is a tribute to the empowerment and comfort derived from Mother Earth and mothers in my past." (26, 40, 54, 63)

**Jean Janzen** teaches poetry writing at Fresno Pacific College. Her own poems have appeared in *Words for the Silence, Three Mennonite Poets*, and in various magazines, journals, and anthologies. She is a member of the College Community Mennonite Brethren Church, Clovis, California. Her husband is Louis Janzen, a pediatrician, and they have four children and three grandchildren. (26, 31, 38, 74, 81)

**Sarah Klassen** is a former English teacher and a poet living in Winnipeg. Her first book of poems, *Journey to Yalta*, was published in 1988. She is a member of the River East Mennonite Brethren Church. (56, 79, 81)

**Ellen Kroeker** is a writer and teacher living in Lawrence, Kansas. (27, 61, 83)

**Nancy S. Lapp** is a counseling elder at Assembly Mennonite Church, Goshen, Indiana. In 1987, she received a master of divinity degree from Associated Mennonite Biblical Seminaries and was ordained by Indiana-Michigan Conference of the Mennonite Church. She is the mother of three young adults in their twenties. (76)

**Cornelia Lehn** was born in Russia and grew up in Saskatchewan. She was an invalid as a young girl but later worked with the Mennonite Central Committee and, then, for many years, with the Commission on Education of the General Conference Mennonite Church, Newton, Kansas. She is now retired and lives in Chilliwack, British Columbia. (15)

**Doris Janzen Longacre** grew up in Elbing, Kansas, and Tucson, Arizona. After earning a degree in home economics from Goshen College, she served with Mennonite Central Committee in Vietnam and Indonesia. She is best known as the compiler of the *More-with-Less Cookbook*. She died in 1979 at the age of thirty-nine. (53, 54)

**Hedy Leonora Martens** began writing during her childhood in Saskatchewan and has continued through marriage, mother/grandmotherhood, and career changes. Publications have been mainly in Mennonite periodicals. She is a family therapist in Winnipeg. Her poem was written in 1982 in London, England. It reflects on the essence of our human struggles which never changes though interpretations of controversial Scriptures do. (75)

**Phyllis Martens**, co-editor of this collection, has a special interest in writing fiction. She teaches English as a second language to international students. With her husband, Elmer, a professor at Mennonite Brethren Biblical Seminary, she has lived and taught in India, China, Africa, and Japan. They have four children. (10)

**Rebecca B. Mast**, State College, Pennsylvania, did her drawings as she worked in a group of artists who shared the expense of a model. Her designs focus on the subject making use of drapery and background. "The creation of an interesting pattern and composition by representing textures, light, and shadow, whatever the subject," she says, "is my goal as I limit myself to the tools of pen and ink." (18, 27, 33, 42, 82)

**Lorraine E. Matties** is a free-lance poet, editor, and mother of two. She and her husband and children live in Winnipeg, Manitoba, where they are active in their small, inner-city Mennonite Brethren church. (47, 82)

**Mary Cender Miller** is an associate professor of English at Hokusei University, Sapporo, Japan. Since 1963, she and her husband, Marvin, have been overseas missions associates in Japan with the Mennonite Board of Missions. (70)

**Ruth Naylor**, Bluffton, Ohio, has published over 100 poems in a variety of religious magazines over the past thirty years. She was an English teacher before becoming associate pastor at First Mennonite Church, Bluffton. A mother of two and grandmother of seven, she is currently president of the Central District Conference. (21, 34, 59, 64)

**Peggy Newcomer**, a long time active member of the Seattle Mennonite Church, worked for three years for Mennonite Central Committee in Cairo, Egypt. She died in April 1989. (20, 77)

**Janice Wiebe Ollenburger** lives in Elkhart, Indiana. "I ask questions. I seek answers. I use tools—brushes, pencils, markers, computers—to express that quest. The results are paintings, drawings, printed pieces. Creating them is the essence of life." (21, 39, 50, 65)

**Margaret Loewen Reimer**, Waterloo, Ontario, is associate editor of *Mennonite Reporter* and a doctoral candidate in English literature at the University of Toronto. She is married to A. James Reimer and is the mother of three children, seven to fifteen years of age. (40)

**Elaine Sommers Rich**, Bluffton, Ohio, has written *Breaking Bread Together*; *Hannah Elizabeth*; *Tomorrow, Tomorrow, Tomorrow*; *Am I This Countryside?*; *Mennonite Women*; *Spiritual Elegance*; and *Prayers for Everyday*. She also writes a fortnightly column for *Mennonite Weekly Review*. (35)

**Anne Neufeld Rupp**, a Canadian, lives in Newton, Kansas. She completed studies at Canadian Mennonite Bible College, Bethel College, and Mennonite Biblical Seminary and received her ARCT from the Royal Conservatory of Toronto. Her published works include poetry, curriculum, and family life articles. She has taught in Mexico, served as co-pastor, and is now coordinator of education/rehabilitation and chaplain at Meadowlark Homestead, a center for persons with long-term mental illness. (46)

**Fern Pankratz Ruth**, North Newton, Kansas, was raised in Moundridge, Kansas, attended Bethel College, married, lived on several central Kansas farms until moving to Wichita. She did clerical work in Wichita hospitals for thirty-five years. Now retired, she has two grown children and three self-published books: *The Stream and All in It*, *Once Summer Came*, and *Of Wonderful Things*. (25, 27)

**Mary H. Schertz**, co-editor of this collection, was born and raised in Illinois. She received a BA in English from Goshen College in 1971 and an MDiv degree from Associated Mennonite Biblical

Seminaries in 1983. After teaching a year at Goshen College, she entered graduate studies in New Testament at Vanderbilt University, and is now completing a dissertation entitled "Questions of the Heart: Feminist Inquiry and Luke's Easter Text." Since 1988, she has been assistant professor of New Testament at AMBS. (10)

**Elizabeth Schmidt** lives in North Newton, Kansas, with her husband Kent Unrau. She works as an advocate for adults with developmental disabilities. Her three poems, she says, "were inspired by my initial encounter with feminist theology and spirituality nearly a decade ago. The vision of a truly inclusive community, sustained by memory and imagination, continues to inspire my faith-journey." (16, 41, 69)

**Kathy Shantz**, Kitchener, Ontario, has a master's degree in German literature and has taught German at the University of Waterloo. She is the mother of a three-year-old daughter and is the part-time director of Women's Concerns for Mennonite Central Committee Canada. (19, 71)

**Barbara Esch Shisler**, Telford, Pennsylvania, is pastor of Indian Creek Foundation, a Mennonite-affiliated agency that serves people with developmental disabilities. Her poems and articles have appeared in religious periodicals and library journals. She is married and has three grown children and one grandchild. (16, 39, 51)

**Muriel Thiessen Stackley**, Newton, Kansas, is just now a parent (of three young adults) and editor (of *The Mennonite*, journal of the General Conference Mennonite Church). For twenty-one years, she was also a wife and is becoming at ease with solitude, assisted in this by her congregation, New Creation Fellowship. (38, 70, 80, 85)

**Shari Miller Wagner** lives in Indianapolis where she teaches part-time at several universities. She has a BA in English from Goshen College and an MFA in creative writing from Indiana University. Her poetry has appeared in various literary magazines. She and her husband, Chuck, attend First Mennonite Church of Indianapolis. (63)

**Judy A. Yoder**, Versailles, Ohio, was born and raised in Elkhart, Indiana. Joining Mennonite Central Committee after graduating from Manchester College in 1975, she taught school in Botswana from 1976 to 1980. An active member of the Church of the Brethren, she teaches art and learning disabilities in Russia, Ohio. A camp counselor during the summers, she enjoys art activities, foreign travel, spelunking, and poetry writing. (80)

**Erma Martin Yost** created the quilt/painting assemblages presented in this book between 1981 and 1984 as part of two series. The first series, "Life Cycle," began with "Beginnings" and progressed through eight stages of a woman's life. The second series, "Endangered," focused on flowers and wildlife which to her are symbols of our fragile environment. (1, 14, 22, 30, 35, 36, 48, 58, 66, 72, 78)

# Our patrons

The publishers gratefully acknowledge the contribution of the Mennonite Central Committee Women's Concerns in envisioning this collection of women's art and encouraging its publication. We further acknowledge the financial support of Women's Concerns, Mennonite Central Committee Manitoba, and the Peace and Social Concerns Committee of Mennonite Central Committee Ontario as well as that of the following special friends of the arts: Jake and Louise Buhler, the DeFehr Foundation, William and Velma Dyck, Leola Epp, Winifred Ewy, Lois Frey, Maggie Glick, Hiram and Mary Jane Hershey, Joyce Hildebrand, Jean Janzen, Marilyn R. Kern, Elona Kreigbaum, Ruth A. Kulp, Lee Hazelton Memorial Fund, Joyce Hildebrand, Cornelia Lehn, Irene Loewen, Cara Longacre, Kelly Loree, Linda Alderfer Martin, Cheryl L. Martin, Lana Lea Miller, Mr. and Mrs. John Nissen, Gary and Christine Wenger Nofsinger, Eileen Pankratz, Peggy Regehr, Janayce Regier, Ruth L. Rittgers, Gloria Horst Rosenberger, Becky Schenck, Milo and Laura Shantz, Barbara Shisler, Muriel Thiessen Stackley, Priscilla and Dennis Stuckey-Kauffman, Bev Suderman, Hildi F. Tiessen, Katie Funk Wiebe, Bob and Lucille Willems, and Doris Zook.